# TOPICAL MEMORY SYSTEM

## Course Workbook

HIDE GOD'S WORD IN YOUR HEART

NavPress

*A NavPress resource published in alliance with Tyndale House Publishers*

NavPress is the publishing ministry of The Navigators, an international Christian organization and leader in personal spiritual development. NavPress is committed to helping people grow spiritually and enjoy lives of meaning and hope through personal and group resources that are biblically rooted, culturally relevant, and highly practical.

**For more information, visit NavPress.com.**

| 26 | 25 | 24 | 23 | 22 | 21 | 20 |
|----|----|----|----|----|----|----|
| 23 | 22 | 21 | 20 | 19 | 18 | 17 |

# CONTENTS

# Versions of the Bible

The *Topical Memory System* contains sixty verses in the following versions: *New International Version* (NIV), *The Message* (MSG), *New American Standard Bible* (NASB), *New King James Version* (NKJV), *English Standard Version* (ESV), *King James Version* (KJV), *New Revised Standard Version* (NRSV), and *New Living Translation* (NLT). The verses are printed on perforated sheets. Please tear out the cards for the version of your choice.

# BEGIN A LIFETIME OF SCRIPTURE MEMORY AND MEDITATION

**Y**ou can memorize Scripture. The process may seem slow at first as you follow the *Topical Memory System* and begin building consistent Scripture memory and meditation into your life. But in the long run, *the system saves you time.* Do your best to form good memory habits now as you follow the weekly plans in this book.

*Attitude makes the difference.* Be confident as you begin memorizing, and you will develop skill.

*You can count on God's help as you memorize.* Remember his counsel — "These commandments that I give you today are to be on your hearts" (Deuteronomy 6:6); and, "Let the message of Christ dwell among you richly" (Colossians 3:16).

**What Scripture Memory Will Do for You**
Memorizing and meditating on God's Word will help you *overcome worry.* You can experience God's perfect peace by knowing his promises and having them written on your heart.

Another benefit is *victory over sin.* The psalmist wrote, "I have hidden your word in my heart that I might not sin against you" (Psalm 119:11). God's Word hidden in your heart is the sword of the Spirit, available for battle at any time against sin and Satan.

Scripture memory will also help you gain *confidence in witnessing.* One of the five series of verses in the *Topical Memory*

*System* (Series B: "Proclaim Christ") will give you a workable plan for sharing the gospel with others.

Scripture memory will help you keep spiritually fit. You will experience immediate benefits and become better equipped to meet future needs and opportunities.

**A Look at the *Topical Memory System***

The *Topical Memory System* is designed to help you learn four things:

1. How to memorize and meditate on Scripture most effectively.
2. How to apply in your life the verses you memorize.
3. How to review the verses so you can always recall them easily.
4. How to continue memorizing Scripture after you finish this course.

The sixty verses of the *Topical Memory System* are arranged in five series:

- Series A — "Live the New Life"
- Series B — "Proclaim Christ"
- Series C — "Rely on God's Resources"
- Series D — "Be Christ's Disciple"
- Series E — "Grow in Christlikeness"

Each series has twelve verses. These verses are arranged according to topics. There are two verses for each topic.

The recommended pace for learning new verses is two verses per week. Since there are two verses for each topic, you can focus on one topic each week.

## Why the Topics?

Two important reasons for knowing the topics of the verses you memorize are:

1. The topics help you understand the meaning of the verses.
2. The topics give you mental "hooks" with which to draw a particular verse from memory when you need it. They help you recall the right verse when studying the Bible, witnessing, or counseling. The topics serve as pegs on which to hang the verses as you learn them.

## Memorize the References

Knowing the reference for each verse you memorize makes it possible to find the verses in the Bible immediately when you need them for personal use or in helping others. So make the reference a part of each verse you memorize.

The surest way to remember the reference is to say it both before and after the verse each time you review it. This will connect the reference and the verse in your mind.

When learning or reviewing a verse, make it a habit to say the topic first, then the reference, then the verse, and the reference again at the end. This may seem tedious at first, but it is important — and it works!

## When Is the Best Time to Memorize?

Memorizing the verses is easiest when you can concentrate without distraction. Two of the best times are just before you go to bed at night and just before or after your morning devotional time. A few minutes at lunchtime or just before supper may also work well for you.

Use spare moments during the day — such as while you wait, walk, or drive — to review your verses. Develop the habit of carrying your verse pack with you.

## Why Learn Word-Perfectly?

Have as your aim to always quote a verse word-perfectly. It is easier to learn verses correctly at first. This also makes it easier to review them later. Knowing them word-perfectly will also give you greater confidence in using your verses.

Once you have chosen a particular Bible translation for the verses you memorize, it is best to learn all your verses in that translation, rather than mixing in others.

## The Verse Cards

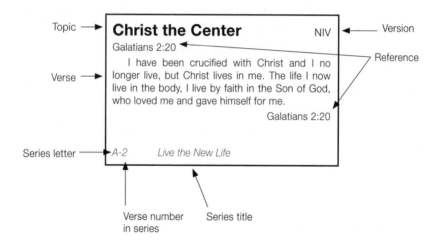

# Checklist: The *Topical Memory System*

Each week place a check next to the reference of the verses you have successfully memorized that week:

## Series A: Live the New Life

| | | |
|---|---|---|
| Christ the Center | ☐ 2 Corinthians 5:17 | ☐ Galatians 2:20 |
| Obedience to Christ | ☐ Romans 12:1 | ☐ John 14:21 |
| God's Word | ☐ 2 Timothy 3:16 | ☐ Joshua 1:8 |
| Prayer | ☐ John 15:7 | ☐ Philippians 4:6-7 |
| Fellowship | ☐ 1 John 1:3 | ☐ Hebrews 10:24-25 |
| Witnessing | ☐ Matthew 4:19 | ☐ Romans 1:16 |

## Series B: Proclaim Christ

| | | |
|---|---|---|
| All Have Sinned | ☐ Romans 3:23 | ☐ Isaiah 53:6 |
| Sin's Penalty | ☐ Romans 6:23 | ☐ Hebrews 9:27 |
| Christ Paid the Penalty | ☐ Romans 5:8 | ☐ 1 Peter 3:18 |
| Salvation Not by Works | ☐ Ephesians 2:8-9 | ☐ Titus 3:5 |
| Must Receive Christ | ☐ John 1:12 | ☐ Revelation 3:20 |
| Assurance of Salvation | ☐ 1 John 5:13 | ☐ John 5:24 |

## Series C: Rely on God's Resources

| | | |
|---|---|---|
| His Spirit | ☐ 1 Corinthians 3:16 | ☐ 1 Corinthians 2:12 |
| His Strength | ☐ Isaiah 41:10 | ☐ Philippians 4:13 |
| His Faithfulness | ☐ Lamentations 3:22-23 | ☐ Numbers 23:19 |
| His Peace | ☐ Isaiah 26:3 | ☐ 1 Peter 5:7 |
| His Provision | ☐ Romans 8:32 | ☐ Philippians 4:19 |
| His Help in Temptation | ☐ Hebrews 2:18 | ☐ Psalm 119:9, 11 |

## Series D: Be Christ's Disciple

| | | |
|---|---|---|
| Put Christ First | ☐ Matthew 6:33 | ☐ Luke 9:23 |
| Separate from the World | ☐ 1 John 2:15-16 | ☐ Romans 12:2 |
| Be Steadfast | ☐ 1 Corinthians 15:58 | ☐ Hebrews 12:3 |
| Serve Others | ☐ Mark 10:45 | ☐ 2 Corinthians 4:5 |
| Give Generously | ☐ Proverbs 3:9-10 | ☐ 2 Corinthians 9:6-7 |
| Develop World Vision | ☐ Acts 1:8 | ☐ Matthew 28:19-20 |

## Series E: Grow in Christlikeness

| | | |
|---|---|---|
| Love | ☐ John 13:34-35 | ☐ 1 John 3:18 |
| Humility | ☐ Philippians 2:3-4 | ☐ 1 Peter 5:5-6 |
| Purity | ☐ Ephesians 5:3 | ☐ 1 Peter 2:11 |
| Honesty | ☐ Leviticus 19:11 | ☐ Acts 24:16 |
| Faith | ☐ Hebrews 11:6 | ☐ Romans 4:20-21 |
| Good Works | ☐ Galatians 6:9-10 | ☐ Matthew 5:16 |

# Live the New Life

Every person has physical life. But when we receive Jesus Christ into our lives as Savior and Lord, we then possess a new, spiritual life — the life of Christ within us.

This new life may be illustrated by a wheel, as you see below. A wheel gets its driving force from the hub. In the Christian life, Christ is the hub — the source of power and motivation for living a Christian life. He lives in us in the person of the Holy Spirit, whose expressed purpose is to glorify Christ (see John 16:13-14).

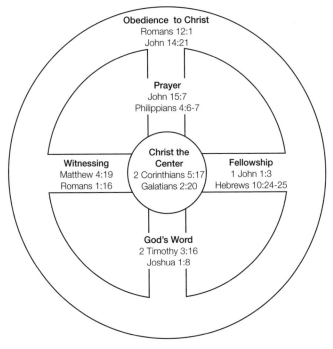

*The rim of the wheel represents you,* the Christian, responding to Christ's lordship through your wholehearted obedience to him. This obedience involves your faithfulness in basic principles of Christian living.

The spokes of the wheel represent these basic principles — the means whereby Christ's power reaches our lives. The vertical spokes concern our relationship to God through the Scriptures and prayer. The horizontal spokes represent our relationships to other people, both believers and unbelievers, through fellowship and witnessing.

The wheel functions smoothly only when all the spokes are present and in proper balance.

# Week 1

**TOPIC:** Christ the Center
**VERSES:** 2 Corinthians 5:17; Galatians 2:20

## Your Plan This Week

- Before beginning to memorize these first two verses, read through the "Principles for Memorizing Scripture" on page 15. Place a check here when you have completed reading this: _____
- Put your name, address, and telephone number on the small identification card. Place this card and the twelve Series A verse cards in your verse pack. (You can put all these cards in only one side of your verse pack for now. As you memorize the verses one by one, use the other side of the pack to hold the cards you have already learned.)
- Use the first two days of the week to memorize 2 Corinthians 5:17, and the third and fourth days to learn Galatians 2:20. Follow the steps outlined on pages 15 and 16.
- Use the remainder of the week to review and meditate on both verses, making sure you know them well before going on to memorize others. You can use the "questions for meditation" to help you understand the verses.
- At the end of the week, check yourself by writing out your verses from memory or quoting them to someone else. Then check off these two verses on the checklist on page 9. (Use this same procedure each week.)

## Questions for Meditation

2 Corinthians 5:17 (context: read 2 Corinthians 5:14-21)

- What is the key to living a truly new life?

- What has happened to your "old" life?
- What things have changed in your life since you became a Christian?

Galatians 2:20 (context: read Galatians 2:17-21)

- How are we identified with Christ in his death?
- If you had a problem with being prideful, how would the truth of this passage help you overcome it?

## Meditation and Review

You can use the space at the end of each weekly plan to record your thoughts as you meditate on your verses, or to write them from memory to check how well you have learned them.

# Principles for Memorizing Scripture

You'll want to refer to these principles often in the coming weeks:

**As You Start to Memorize a Verse**
1. Be sure to read and follow each week the plans given in this book for memorizing the verses. Following this plan will help you gain more than a shallow understanding of the verses as you learn them.
2. Read in your Bible the context of each verse you memorize.
3. Try to gain a clear understanding of what each verse actually means. (You may want to read the verse in other Bible translations or paraphrases to get a better grasp of the meaning.)
4. Read the verse through several times thoughtfully, aloud or in a whisper. This will help you grasp the verse as a whole. Each time you read it, say the topic, reference, verse, and then the reference again.
5. Discuss the verse with God in prayer, and continue to seek his help for success in Scripture memory.

**While You Are Memorizing the Verse**
6. Work on saying the verse aloud as much as possible.
7. Learn the topic and reference first.
8. After learning the topic and reference, learn the first phrase of the verse. Once you have learned the topic, reference, and first phrase and have repeated them several times, continue adding more phrases after you can quote correctly what you have already learned.
9. Think about how the verse applies to you and your daily circumstances.

10. Always include the topic and reference as part of the verse as you learn and review it.

**After You Can Quote Correctly the Topic, Reference, Verse, and Reference Again**

11. It is helpful to write the verse out. This deepens the impression in your mind.
12. Review the verse immediately after learning it, and repeat it frequently in the next few days. This is crucial for getting the verse firmly fixed in mind because of how quickly we tend to forget something recently learned.
13. REVIEW! REVIEW! REVIEW! Repetition is the best way to engrave the verses on your memory.

# Week 2

**TOPIC:** Obedience to Christ
**VERSES:** Romans 12:1; John 14:21

## Your Plan This Week

- Read "How to Review Memory Verses with Someone Else" on page 19. Check here when you have completed reading it: _____
- Follow the same pattern for learning new verses as you did last week — use the first two days of the week to learn Romans 12:1, and the next two days to learn John 14:21. Review both of these verses during the rest of the week to deepen your grasp of them.
- Carry your verse pack with you and use spare moments during the day for review and meditation.
- At the end of the week, check yourself as you did before by writing out your new verses from memory, or quoting them to someone else.
- DAILY REVIEW: Each day this week, review the first two verses in Series A: 2 Corinthians 5:17 and Galatians 2:20.

## Questions for Meditation

Romans 12:1 (context: read Romans 11:32–12:2)
- What is the right motivation for yielding ourselves to God?
- What is sacrifice?
- What is worship?

John 14:21 (context: John 14:15-21)
- What is the proof of our love for God?
- According to this verse, what responsibilities do you have?
- In what ways do you feel a desire to express your love to the Lord?

## Meditation and Review

---

Remember that Scripture memory is not an end in itself. It must be followed by prayerful meditation and by obedience and application.

- *Scripture memory* puts God's Word on your *mind*.
- *Prayerful meditation* puts God's Word in your *heart*.
- *Obedience* puts God's Word into *action*.

---

# How to Review Memory Verses with Someone Else

1. Follow this procedure: One person holds the other person's verse cards and calls out the topic and reference of the first card. The other person then repeats the topic and reference and goes on to quote the entire verse and the reference again at the end. Then go on to other cards in the same way.
2. First review the memory verses you know best.
3. Speak your verses clearly and not too rapidly so you can be easily understood.
4. While the other person is quoting his verses, be helpful and encouraging. Do all you can to ensure his success.
5. When the other person makes a mistake, signal this to him by shaking your head or saying no. Give him verbal help only if he asks you.
6. Once the other person has realized his mistake, have him repeat the entire verse word-perfectly before going on.
7. Make it your absolute goal to repeat each verse word-perfectly.

Memorizing and reviewing Scripture with one or more friends will provide mutual encouragement, as well as opportunities to discuss difficulties in memorization. You will also be helped by having someone with whom to share how God is using the verses in your life.

# Week 3

**TOPIC:** God's Word
**VERSES:** 2 Timothy 3:16; Joshua 1:8

## Your Plan This Week

- Follow the same pattern — spend the first two days of the week learning 2 Timothy 3:16, and the next two days on Joshua 1:8. Use the rest of the week for review. Remember to check yourself.
- Remember that it is helpful to write out the verse while you are trying to deepen its impression on your mind.
- DAILY REVIEW: Each day this week, review the four verses you have already learned.

## Questions for Meditation

2 Timothy 3:16 (context: 2 Timothy 3:14-17)
- Who is the author of the Scriptures?
- Notice the order of the four benefits of Scripture listed in this verse. What significance do you see in this order?

Joshua 1:8 (context: Joshua 1:6-9)
- What is the purpose of meditation?
- What kind of prosperity and success do you think this verse refers to?

## Meditation and Review

# Week 4

**TOPIC:** Prayer
**VERSES:** John 15:7; Philippians 4:6-7

## Your Plan This Week
- As you learn and meditate on these new verses, plan to set aside a special time of prayer this week, with the principles from these verses fresh in your mind.
- DAILY REVIEW: Each day this week, review the six verses you have learned in Series A.

## Questions for Meditation
John 15:7 (context: John 15:5-8)
- What to you is the most important part of this verse? Why?
- Who is speaking these words?
- What does this verse tell us about Christ's character?

Philippians 4:6-7 (context: Philippians 4:4-9)
- In what situations are we to pray?
- How does this passage relate to Colossians 3:15?
- What kind of protection does God's inner peace provide us?

## Meditation and Review

# Week 5

**Topic:** Fellowship
**Verses:** 1 John 1:3; Hebrews 10:24-25

## Your Plan This Week
- To establish a good habit that will last a lifetime takes time and careful effort. Follow consistently each week the pattern you have learned in earlier weeks for memorizing new verses.
- Remember to read in your Bible the context of each verse you memorize.
- As you learn these verses on fellowship, evaluate the amount of time you spend with other Christians, and the quality of that time. Does it meet biblical standards?
- DAILY REVIEW: The first eight verses in Series A.

## Questions for Meditation
1 John 1:3 (context: 1 John 1:1-4)
- How do you think fellowship with the body of Christ invites us into further fellowship with God?

Hebrews 10:24-25 (context: Hebrews 10:19-25)
- What encourages you to love and to do good deeds?
- Verse 25 speaks of "the Day," which refers to the day of Christ's return. In what ways do you see this day approaching?

## Meditation and Review

# Week 6

**Topic:** Witnessing
**Verses:** Matthew 4:19; Romans 1:16

## Your Plan This Week

- Who are the non-Christians in your life with whom you would like to share your faith in Christ? You may want to make a list of these persons and use the list to pray for them and to plan for opportunities to talk with them.
- DAILY REVIEW: The first ten verses in Series A. Your goal should be to repeat each verse once a day. However, the more time you spend on your verses, the more you will profit.

## Questions for Meditation

Matthew 4:19 (context: Matthew 4:18-22)

- What part of this verse is a command, and what part is a promise?
- Who were these words spoken to, and how did they respond?

Romans 1:16 (context: Romans 1:11-17)

- How does this verse show that the gospel is for all people?
- How would you define in your own words the power of the gospel?

## Meditation and Review

# Proclaim Christ

As witnesses for Jesus Christ we have two things to share — our testimony of how we found Christ and what He means to us, and the gospel, God's plan of salvation. The gospel includes the facts of man's need, God's love for man, and what He did to meet that need.

The references of the verses you will learn in Series B are shown below in a diagram illustrating how Christ is mankind's bridge from death to life.

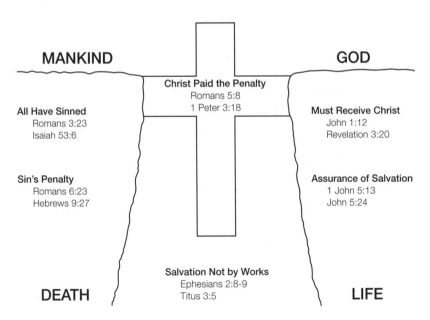

**MANKIND**     **GOD**

**Christ Paid the Penalty**
Romans 5:8
1 Peter 3:18

**All Have Sinned**
Romans 3:23
Isaiah 53:6

**Must Receive Christ**
John 1:12
Revelation 3:20

**Sin's Penalty**
Romans 6:23
Hebrews 9:27

**Assurance of Salvation**
1 John 5:13
John 5:24

**Salvation Not by Works**
Ephesians 2:8-9
Titus 3:5

**DEATH**     **LIFE**

# Week 7

**Topic:** All Have Sinned
**Verses:** Romans 3:23; Isaiah 53:6

## Your Plan This Week

- Review again the "Principles for Memorizing Scripture" on page 15 to see if there are any principles you are overlooking. Place a check here when you have reviewed these principles:____
- Follow the same pattern in learning the Series B verses as you did in memorizing Series A. At the end of the week, remember to check yourself by writing out your new verses from memory or quoting them to someone else.
- DAILY REVIEW: All twelve verses of Series A. (You can keep the Series A cards in one side of your verse pack, and Series B in the other.)

## Questions for Meditation

Romans 3:23 (context: Romans 3:21-26)

- Can you think of any problem people experience today that cannot be traced back to the human condition described in this verse?

Isaiah 53:6 (context: Isaiah 53:4-9)

- Why are we responsible for our sin?
- How does this verse show that Christ's crucifixion was part of God's plan?

## Meditation and Review

# Week 8

**TOPIC:** Sin's Penalty
**VERSES:** Romans 6:23; Hebrews 9:27

## Your Plan This Week

- Read "How to Meditate on the Scriptures" (page 28), and place a check here when you have completed reading it:
  ____

- DAILY REVIEW: Series A, plus the first two verses in Series B.

## Questions for Meditation

Romans 6:23 (context: Romans 6:19-23)
- How does this verse reflect both God's love and his judgment?

Hebrews 9:27 (context: Hebrews 9:24-28)
- What is the relationship between the facts that man dies only once (verse 27) and that Christ died only once (verse 28)?

## Meditation and Review

# How to Meditate on the Scriptures

Meditation is not mind wandering. Meditation has a form and an object. It is directing our thoughts to a single topic. Meditation is thinking with a purpose.

Meditation is not a solemn, academic exercise. It requires an attitude of curiosity and expectation, and leads to exciting discoveries, a refreshed spirit, and transformation of character. It brings reward and benefit. It is a crucial step toward fully knowing and obeying God's will.

Here are five methods of meditation you may want to try:

1. Paraphrasing. Some exciting insights can come from rewriting a verse or passage in your own words. This exercise is made even more challenging by using as few words as possible in your paraphrase.

    For example, Isaiah 26:3 reads:

    > You will keep in perfect peace
    >    those whose minds are steadfast,
    >    because they trust in you.

    You could paraphrase this, "You promise freedom from worry to the person who trusts you completely without any doubts in his mind."

2. Asking questions. You can sort through the information in a verse by asking who, what, where, why, and how questions about the verse, or by jotting down random questions that come to mind as you memorize and reflect on it. (You may not come up with answers for all your questions.)

For Isaiah 26:3 you could ask, "Who does God give perfect peace to?" "What attitude toward God do I need to have in my mind?" and "Why does God provide this perfect peace?"

3. Praying. Pray over the passage: Praise God for the way his character is revealed in the verse; thank him for any promises you see, and claim these in your own life; and confess any failure which the verse may bring to mind.

   Think "out loud" with God as you meditate.

4. Emphasizing different words or phrases. This simple exercise involves fixing your focus on small parts of the verse and how they relate to the verse as a whole.

   For Isaiah 26:3, you could emphasize these words and think of their implications: "You will keep in perfect peace," "You will keep in perfect peace," "You will keep in perfect peace," and so on.

5. Finding cross-references. Try to think of other passages that relate directly to the meaning of the verse you are memorizing. Looking for the relationships between various parts of Scripture can be stimulating and will help you gain an overall view of the major themes in God's Word.

   Again considering Isaiah 26:3, you might think of Philippians 4:6-7, 1 Peter 5:7, or Matthew 11:28.

   In all these forms of meditation, relate the verse to your own circumstances. Suppose you are worried and restless and are not experiencing inner peace. You know this doesn't please the Lord, but you can't help it. You decide to meditate on Isaiah 26:3 as a source of help.

   As you think about the verse, you ask yourself, "What does it mean to have perfect peace? Is this really available to me? How can I trust God more?"

Then you might make a list of the things that trouble you. For each item on the list you ask, "Am I ready to trust God to take care of these things for me? Am I willing to make a conscious effort to really trust him?"

Some Christians confuse Bible knowledge with spiritual maturity, assuming that knowing more about the Bible automatically makes them better Christians. This is not true. The Pharisees knew the Old Testament, yet they were spiritual reprobates. The key to spiritual maturity is applying God's Word to your life.

# Week 9

**TOPIC:** Christ Paid the Penalty
**VERSES:** Romans 5:8; 1 Peter 3:18

## Your Plan This Week
- DAILY REVIEW: Series A, plus the first four verses in Series B.

## Questions for Meditation
Romans 5:8 (context: Romans 5:6-11)
- From this passage, how would you describe true love?

1 Peter 3:18 (context: 1 Peter 3:13-22)
- Why did Christ die for us?
- How does this verse relate to Jesus' cry on the cross recorded in Matthew 27:46?

## Meditation and Review

# Week 10

**Topic:** Salvation Not by Works
**Verses:** Ephesians 2:8-9; Titus 3:5

## Your Plan This Week

- DAILY REVIEW: Series A, plus the first six verses in Series B.

## Questions for Meditation

Ephesians 2:8-9 (context: Ephesians 2:4-10)

- Why can a Christian never truthfully say, "I am a self-made man"?
- How should the truth of this passage affect the way we live once we have accepted God's gift of salvation?

Titus 3:5 (context: Titus 3:3-8)

- What does this passage show about God's character?

## Meditation and Review

# Week 11

**TOPIC:** Must Receive Christ
**VERSES:** John 1:12; Revelation 3:20

## Your Plan This Week
- DAILY REVIEW: Series A, and the first eight verses in Series B.

## Questions for Meditation
John 1:12 (context: John 1:10-14)
- To whom does God give the right to become his children?
- In your opinion, what benefits are associated with being someone's son or daughter?

Revelation 3:20 (context: Revelation 3:14-22)
- How does this verse illustrate faith?
- What two things does Christ do if we allow him into our lives?

## Meditation and Review

# Week 12

**Topic:** Assurance of Salvation
**Verses:** 1 John 5:13; John 5:24

## Your Plan This Week

- DAILY REVIEW: Series A, plus all the verses learned in Series B.

## Questions for Meditation

1 John 5:13 (context: 1 John 5:9-15)

- What was John's primary objective in writing these words?
- What should we rely on when we are tempted to doubt what Christ has done for us?

John 5:24 (context: John 5:16-30)

- What two things are required to receive the blessings Jesus mentions here?
- How do these blessings relate to our past, our present, and our future?

## Meditation and Review

The more meaningful a verse is to you, the easier it is to remember. That's why it is important to read each verse in its context and understand it before you memorize it. You will also want to pray about the things mentioned in the verse.

# Rely on God's Resources

God "has given us everything we need for a godly life" (2 Peter 1:3). These blessings come to us "through our knowledge of him who called us by his own glory and goodness" (1:3).

Knowing our limitations and knowing every trial and test we will ever face, the Lord has provided all we need to live victoriously and fruitfully for his glory.

Our part is to commit ourselves to him, to get to know him well, to appropriate his resources, and to obey him completely. He will provide the strength and ability. "For God is at work within you, helping you want to obey him, and then helping you do what he wants" (Philippians 2:13, TLB).

In Series C are six spiritual resources you can rely on to enable you to fulfill God's will for your life:

- His Spirit — 1 Corinthians 3:16 and 1 Corinthians 2:12
- His Strength — Isaiah 41:10 and Philippians 4:13
- His Faithfulness — Lamentations 3:22-23 and Numbers 23:19
- His Peace — Isaiah 26:3 and 1 Peter 5:7
- His Provision — Romans 8:32 and Philippians 4:19
- His Help in Temptation — Hebrews 2:18 and Psalm 119:9, 11

# Week 13

**Topic:** His Spirit
**Verses:** 1 Corinthians 3:16; 1 Corinthians 2:12

## Your Plan This Week

- With daily practice you already have learned important principles for effective Scripture memory and review. Continue to build these habits into your life. You may want to look over again the "Principles for Memorizing Scripture" on page 15.
- DAILY REVIEW: All the verses in Series B.

## Questions for Meditation

1 Corinthians 3:16 (context: 1 Corinthians 3:1-23)

- What do you know about the temple in the Old Testament that can help you better understand this verse?
- How is the teaching of this verse extended further in 1 Corinthians 6:19–20?

1 Corinthians 2:12 (context: 1 Corinthians 2:6-16)

- What has God freely given us?
- What does this verse tell us about the work of the Holy Spirit?

## Meditation and Review

# Week 14

**TOPIC:** His Strength
**VERSES:** Isaiah 41:10; Philippians 4:13

## Your Plan This Week
- DAILY REVIEW: Series B, plus the first two verses in Series C.

## Questions for Meditation
Isaiah 41:10 (context: Isaiah 41:8-10)
- What promises does God give to Israel in this verse?
- What does this passage tell about the kind of relationship God wants to have with his people?

Philippians 4:13 (context: Philippians 4:10-13)
- How is the statement in this verse related to what Paul says in Philippians 4:11 — "I have learned to be content whatever the circumstances"?
- How does the truth of this passage relate to Paul's statement in 2 Corinthians 3:4-5?
- What is some situation in your life in which you need to rely on God's strength?

## Meditation and Review

# Week 15

**TOPIC:** His Faithfulness
**VERSES:** Lamentations 3:22-23; Numbers 23:19

## Your Plan This Week
- Once you learn the verses for this topic, you will be halfway through the *Topical Memory System*. To review what you have learned about Scripture memory principles so far, take the self-checking quiz on page 39.
- DAILY REVIEW: Series B, plus the first four verses in Series C. Also, review all of Series A at least once this week.

## Questions for Meditation
Lamentations 3:22-23 (context: Lamentations 3:19-33)
- What evidence does God give us of his love for us?
- What convinces you of God's faithfulness?

Numbers 23:19 (context: Numbers 23:13-26)
- How can the truth of this passage increase our faith?
- How would you restate this verse in your own words?

## Meditation and Review

# Self-Checking Quiz

This quiz will help you check your grasp of Scripture memory principles. After answering the questions, compare your answers with those listed at the end of the quiz.

1. Your success in memorizing Scripture depends entirely on your own ability and confidence. (True or false? Circle your answer.)

   T             F

2. Learning the topics with the verses . . . (Check the best answer.)
   ___ a. is optional in the *Topical Memory System*.
   ___ b. gives you mental hooks with which you can draw a particular verse from memory when you need it.
   ___ c. is a good mental exercise because it makes learning the verses more difficult.

3. It is best to learn the verses word-perfectly because this . . . (Check the *two* best answers.)
   ___ a. will give you greater confidence in using your verses.
   ___ b. makes it easier both to learn verses initially and to review them later.
   ___ c. impresses others with your knowledge of Scripture.

4. The verses in Series A deal with the essential elements of the obedient, Christ-centered life.

   T             F

5. In which aspect of the Christian life are the verses in Series B most helpful?
   ___ a. Knowing the will of God.
   ___ b. Fellowship.
   ___ c. Knowing how to witness to non-Christians.
   ___ d. Knowing how to overcome anxiety.
   ___ e. Prayer.

6. Why is it helpful to memorize and review Scripture with one or more friends? (Check three best answers.)
   ___ a. It provides mutual encouragement.
   ___ b. You can show others how well you are doing.
   ___ c. It provides opportunities to discuss difficulties in memorization.
   ___ d. It allows you to compare yourself with others.
   ___ e. You have someone with whom to share how God is using the verses in your life.

7. A first step toward knowing and obeying God's will is to . . . (Check the correct answer.)
   ___ a. first straighten out your life as best you can.
   ___ b. know a lot about the Bible.
   ___ c. meditate on the Scriptures.

**Correct answers:**

1 — F; 2 — b; 3 — a and b; 4 — T; 5 — c; 6 — a, c, and e; 7 — c.

# Week 16

**Topic:** His Peace
**Verses:** Isaiah 26:3; 1 Peter 5:7

**Your Plan This Week:**
- DAILY REVIEW: Series B, plus the first six verses in Series C.

**Questions for Meditation**
Isaiah 26:3 (context: Isaiah 26:1-11)
- What does trusting God result in?
- How does the truth of this verse relate to Philippians 4:6-7?

1 Peter 5:7 (context: 1 Peter 5:1-11)
- What seems to prevent us from experiencing more of God's peace?
- From the context of this verse, what is the relationship between humility and knowing God's peace?
- What anxieties are you currently experiencing?

**Meditation and Review**

# Week 17

**Topic:** His Provision
**Verses:** Romans 8:32; Philippians 4:19

### Your Plan This Week
- Read "Two Essentials in Scripture Memory" and "If Your Scripture Memory Work Becomes Too Routine" (page 43).
- DAILY REVIEW: Series B, plus the first eight verses in Series C.

### Questions for Meditation
Romans 8:32 (context: Romans 8:28-39)
- How committed is God to your well-being?
- As you think about your future, what foundational truth can this verse provide?

Philippians 4:19 (context: Philippians 4:10-20)
- From the context of this verse, what action of the Philippians prompted Paul to make his statement in verse 19?
- What is the difference, in your opinion, between a need and a desire?

### Meditation and Review

# Two Essentials in Scripture Memory

Two rules from the foundation for a successful Scripture memory program:

1. Consistently memorize new verses each week.
2. Follow a regular, daily program of reviewing the verses you have already memorized.

If at the end of a particular week you cannot quote word-perfectly the verses you intended to memorize that week, you may be tempted to think, *I won't memorize any new verses next week, but instead will concentrate on learning these before resuming work on new verses.*

But skipping one week makes it easier to skip another, and then another. Instead, you should memorize new verses as usual, and put extra effort into learning any verses you have missed. Ask for God's help.

# If Your Scripture Memory Work Becomes Too Routine

Don't get discouraged if your Scripture memory work begins to seem too routine. The process of recording Scripture on your mind and heart does have a mechanical aspect. It requires certain methods and a great deal of perseverance. But as long as the process of imprinting God's Word on your heart is moving forward, these Scriptures will be continually available for life-giving work.

There are helpful things you can do, however, if your Scripture memory program begins to seem lifeless. Try spending more time going over your verses in prayer and meditation. Also begin using the verses in your conversations or in letters. New freshness can come through sharing the Scriptures with others.

Keep in mind that memorizing and meditating on the Scriptures is a practical way of making them available to the Holy Spirit to use in your life.

# Week 18

**TOPIC:** His Help in Temptation
**VERSES:** Hebrews 2:18; Psalm 119:9, 11

## Your Plan This Week
- DAILY REVIEW: Series B, plus the first ten verses in Series C. Also, review all of Series A at least once this week.

## Questions for Meditation
Hebrews 2:18 (context: Hebrews 2:10-18)
- How does the truth of this passage relate to John 1:14?
- What benefits come to us because of Christ's temptation?

Psalm 119:9, 11 (context: Psalm 119:9-16)
- In regard to sin, does this passage relate more to correction or to prevention?
- Can you say honestly that you are living according to God's Word? Why or why not?

## Meditation and Review

# Be Christ's Disciple

Except for His redemptive work on the cross, Jesus Christ's most important work on earth was raising up a band of dedicated disciples who would multiply themselves and make an impact on the world.

Jesus ministered to the multitudes, but at times He purposefully left them. He sometimes seemed to discourage people from following him. Jesus was not interested in nominal followers, but in truly committed disciples who had counted the cost and on whom He could depend.

Series D presents six imperatives that characterize the kind of disciples Jesus seeks:

- Put Christ First — Matthew 6:33 and Luke 9:23
- Separate from the World — 1 John 2:15-16 and Romans 12:2
- Be Steadfast — 1 Corinthians 15:58 and Hebrews 12:3
- Serve Others — Mark 10:45 and 2 Corinthians 4:5
- Give Generously — Proverbs 3:9-10 and 2 Corinthians 9:6-7
- Develop World Vision — Acts 1:8 and Matthew 28:19-20

# Week 19

**TOPIC:** Put Christ First
**VERSES:** Matthew 6:33; Luke 9:23

## Your Plan This Week
- Complete the topic and reference quiz on page 49.
- DAILY REVIEW: All of Series A and C.

## Questions for Meditation
Matthew 6:33 (context: Matthew 6:25-34)
- What are the definitions for righteousness and the kingdom of God? (You may want to use a dictionary and a Bible dictionary or Bible encyclopedia in defining these terms.)

Luke 9:23 (context: Luke 9:18-27)
- From this passage, what seems to be the greatest hindrance to our following Christ?

**• How does this passage reflect the freedom of choice which the Lord gives us in deciding whether we want to follow him? Meditation and Review**

# Topic and Reference Quiz

For each of these topics in Series A, B, and C, fill in the blanks with the correct references.

A. Live the New Life

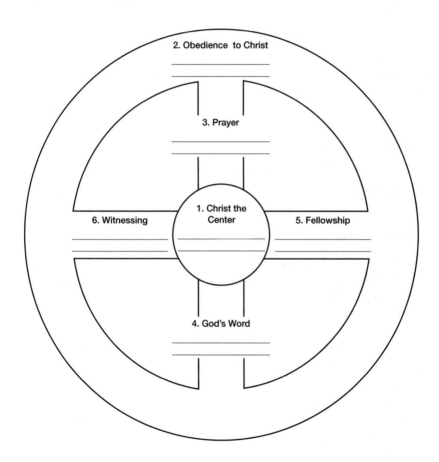

## B. Proclaim Christ

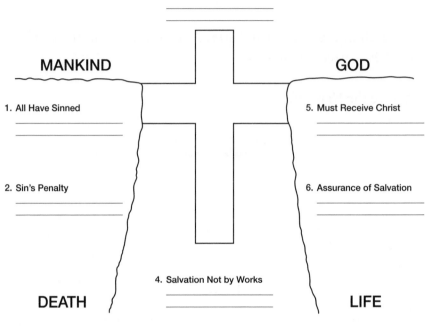

**3. Christ Paid the Penalty**

**MANKIND**          **GOD**

**1. All Have Sinned**          **5. Must Receive Christ**

**2. Sin's Penalty**          **6. Assurance of Salvation**

**4. Salvation Not by Works**

**DEATH**          **LIFE**

## C. Rely on God's Resources

   1. His Spirit

   2. His Strength

   3. His Faithfulness

   4. His Peace

   5. His Provision

   6. His Help in Temptation

# Week 20

**Topic:** Separate from the World
**Verses:** 1 John 2:15-16; Romans 12:2

## Your Plan This Week

- DAILY REVIEW: Series B and C, plus the first two verses in Series D.

## Questions for Meditation

1 John 2:15-16 (context: 1 John 2:12-17)

- How would you define *world* as it is used in this passage?
- If something is not from God, where is it from?

Romans 12:2 (context: Romans 11:32–12:2)

- What pressures should we recognize in the world around us?
- Why do you think our minds have to be transformed before we can recognize God's will?

## Meditation and Review

# Week 21

**Topic:** Be Steadfast
**Verses:** 1 Corinthians 15:58; Hebrews 12:3

## Your Plan This Week
- DAILY REVIEW: Series A and C, plus the first four verses in Series D.

## Questions for Meditation
1 Corinthians 15:58 (context: 1 Corinthians 15:50-58)
- Why do you think Christians need to be encouraged to persevere?
- What should give us confidence as we persevere in the Lord's work?

Hebrews 12:3 (context: Hebrews 12:1-13)
- How would you summarize the opposition Jesus endured from sinful men?
- What are practical ways you can think about Christ when you are tempted to become disheartened?

## Meditation and Review

# Week 22

**Topic:** Serve Others
**Verses:** Mark 10:45; 2 Corinthians 4:5

## Your Plan This Week
- DAILY REVIEW: Series B and C, plus the first six verses in Series D.

## Questions for Meditation
Mark 10:45 (context: Mark 10:35-45)
- In what ways did Jesus serve people?
- What are some specific ways you can follow Jesus' example as a servant?

2 Corinthians 4:5 (context: 2 Corinthians 4:1-18)
- What do you think preaching Jesus Christ as Lord includes?
- What does it mean to serve someone for Jesus' sake?

## Meditation and Review

# Week 23

**TOPIC:** Give Generously
**VERSES:** Proverbs 3:9-10; 2 Corinthians 9:6-7

## Your Plan This Week

- Complete the topic and reference quiz on page 55.
- DAILY REVIEW: Series A and C, plus the first eight verses in Series D.

## Questions for Meditation

Proverbs 3:9-10 (context: Proverbs 3:1-12)

- Why do you think the Lord is honored when we give to him the first part of our material possessions?
- What does this verse show about God's control over our lives?

2 Corinthians 9:6-7 (context: 2 Corinthians 9:6-15)

- Why do you think it is important to God that we not give reluctantly or under compulsion?

## Meditation and Review

# Topic and Reference Quiz

Fill in the blanks with both the correct topics and the correct references for Series A, B, and C.

A. Live the New Life

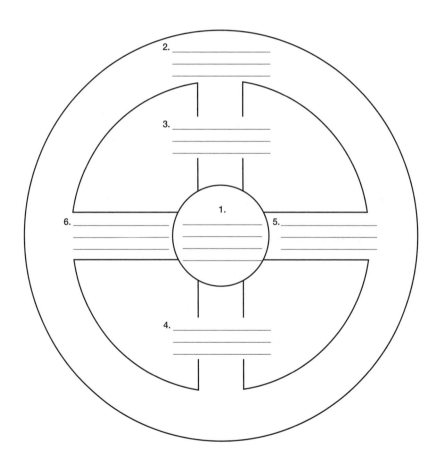

B. Proclaim Christ

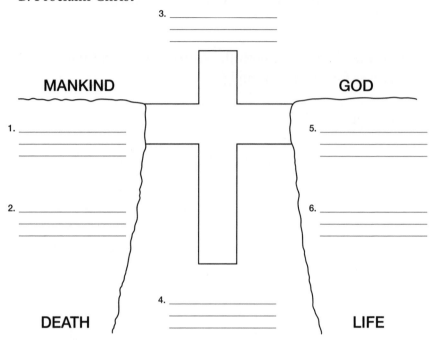

3. _____
   _____
   _____

MANKIND                    GOD

1. _____        5. _____
   _____           _____
   _____           _____

2. _____        6. _____
   _____           _____
   _____           _____

                4. _____
                   _____
DEATH              _____          LIFE

C. Rely on God's Resources

1. _____
   _____          _____

2. _____
   _____          _____

3. _____
   _____          _____

4. _____
   _____          _____

5. _____
   _____          _____

6. _____
   _____          _____

# Week 24

**TOPIC:** Develop World Vision
**VERSES:** Acts 1:8; Matthew 28:19-20

## Your Plan This Week

- DAILY REVIEW: Series B and C, plus the first ten verses in Series D.

## Questions for Meditation

Acts 1:8 (context: Acts 1:1-11)

- What two promises does Jesus make in this verse?
- How are these promises related to each other?

Matthew 28:19-20 (context: Matthew 28:16-20)

- What activities are included in this command of Jesus?
- What part does this command have in your purpose in life?

## Meditation and Review

# Grow in Christlikeness

The Christlike life is the only life that can bring glory to God. Jesus Christ in our lives makes us different, and attracts the attention of others who are searching for reality.

Christlikeness is God's goal for every believer. But many of us have yielded to the pressures to conform to this world by letting non-Christian standards and practices determine our conduct. No wonder our influence for Christ is often small!

Only as others see Jesus Christ in us will they be attracted to him. Christlike character cannot, however, be tacked on the outside; it must spring from within.

As we meditate on Scripture and allow it to permeate our minds, it remains there to influence our reactions and decisions — and to form Christian character. In Series E you will learn twelve passages to help you focus attention on this process:

- Love — John 13:34-35 and 1 John 3:18
- Humility — Philippians 2:3-4 and 1 Peter 5:5-6
- Purity — Ephesians 5:3 and 1 Peter 2:11
- Honesty — Leviticus 19:11 and Acts 24:16
- Faith — Hebrews 11:6 and Romans 4:20-21
- Good Works — Galatians 6:9-10 and Matthew 5:16

# Week 25

**Topic:** Love
**Verses:** John 13:34-35; 1 John 3:18

## Your Plan This Week

- DAILY REVIEW: Series A and D.

## Questions for Meditation

John 13:34-35 (context: John 13:31-38)

- Whose example of love are we to follow?
- How would you describe the way He loved?
- What is the result when we practice this kind of love?

1 John 3:18 (context: 1 John 3:11-24)

- How should we express love?
- How does the truth of this passage relate to 1 Corinthians 13:4-7?

## Meditation and Review

# Week 26

**Topic:** Humility
**Verses:** Philippians 2:3-4; 1 Peter 5:5-6

## Your Plan This Week
- DAILY REVIEW: Series B and D, plus the first two verses in Series E.

## Questions for Meditation
Philippians 2:3-4 (context: Philippians 2:1-11)
- What does this passage imply about being competitive?
- What two motives for action are we to avoid completely?

1 Peter 5:5-6 (context: 1 Peter 5:1-11)
- Is humility more a matter of action or a matter of attitude?
- How can you "humble yourself"?

## Meditation and Review

# Week 27

**Topic:** Purity
**Verses:** Ephesians 5:3; 1 Peter 2:11

## Your Plan This Week
- Take the self-checking quiz on page 63.
- DAILY REVIEW: Series C and D, plus the first four verses in Series E.

## Questions for Meditation
Ephesians 5:3 (context: Ephesians 4:17–5:21)
- What three sins are prohibited in this verse?
- Why are these sins wrong?

1 Peter 2:11 (context: 1 Peter 2:9-12)
- What effect do sinful desires have on us?
- What does it mean to you to be an alien and a stranger in the world?

## Meditation and Review

# Self-Checking Quiz

1. Two essentials for a successful Scripture memory program are . . . (Check the *two* best answers.)
   ___ a. jotting down references of verses you want to learn later.
   ___ b. marking memorized verses in your Bible.
   ___ c. consistently memorizing new verses each week.
   ___ d. following a regular, daily program of reviewing verses you have learned.

2. If memorizing new verses ever becomes routine or lifeless, these things could be done: (Check the *two* best answers.)
   ___ a. Stop memorizing for a month to six weeks.
   ___ b. Spend more time praying over and meditating on your verses.
   ___ c. Find a new way of memorizing.
   ___ d. Begin using the verses more in conversation and in letters.

3. Indicate with letters (A–E) the proper order of the five series of verses in the *Topical Memory System.*
   ___ Rely on God's Resources
   ___ Grow in Christlikeness
   ___ Proclaim Christ
   ___ Live the New Life
   ___ Be Christ's Disciple

4. Add the missing information in this outline of the first four series in the *Topical Memory System*:

A. Live the New Life

   1. Christ the Center

      _____

      Galatians 2:20

   2. Obedience to Christ
      Romans 12:1

      _____

   3. _____
      2 Timothy 3:16

      _____

   4. Prayer

      _____

      Philippians 4:6-7

   5. Fellowship

      _____

      _____

   6. Witnessing
      Matthew 4:19

      _____

B. Proclaim Christ

   1. _____
      Romans 3:23

      _____

   2. _____

      _____

      Hebrews 9:27

3. Christ Paid the Penalty

   _____

   1 Peter 3:18

4. _____

   Ephesians 2:8-9
   Titus 3:5

5. Must Receive Christ

   _____

   Revelation 3:20

6. _____

   _____

   John 5:24

C. Rely on God's Resources

   1. His Spirit

      _____

      _____

   2. His Strength
      Isaiah 41:10

      _____

   3. _____

      _____

      Numbers 23:19

   4. His Peace
      Isaiah 26:3

      _____

5. His Provision
   Romans 8:32

   _____

6. _____
   Hebrews 2:18

   _____

D. Be Christ's Disciple

   1. Put Christ First

      _____

      Luke 9:23

   2. _____

      _____

      Romans 12:2

   3. Be Steadfast
      1 Corinthians 15:58

      _____

   4. Serve Others

      _____

      _____

   5. _____

      _____

      2 Corinthians 9:6-7

   6. _____
      Acts 1:8

      _____

**Correct answers:**

1 — c and d; 2 — b and d; 3 — C, E, B, A, and D; 4 — see the checklist on page 9.

# Week 28

**Topic:** Honesty
**Verses:** Leviticus 19:11; Acts 24:16

## Your Plan This Week

- DAILY REVIEW: Series A and D, plus the first six verses in Series E.

## Questions for Meditation

Leviticus 19:11 (context: Leviticus 19:1-37)

- What three forms of dishonesty are forbidden in this verse?
- Which one of these three sins is most difficult in your life to control?

Acts 24:16 (context: Acts 24:1-27)

- How important is our conscience?
- Is it possible to have a clear conscience toward man but not toward God?

## Meditation and Review

# Week 29

**Topic:** Faith
**Verses:** Hebrews 11:6; Romans 4:20-21

## Your Plan This Week
- DAILY REVIEW: Series B and D, plus the first eight verses in Series E.

## Questions for Meditation
Hebrews 11:6 (context: Hebrews 11:1-40)
- How does the truth of this verse relate to Hebrews 11:1?
- Is it possible to believe God exists, and yet not believe that He rewards those who earnestly seek him? Why or why not?

Romans 4:20-21 (context: Romans 4:1-25)
- What do you know about Abraham that illustrates the truth of this verse?
- What seemed to be the most important factor in Abraham's faith?

## Meditation and Review

# Week 30

**TOPIC:** Good Works
**VERSES:** Galatians 6:9-10; Matthew 5:16

## Your Plan This Week

- DAILY REVIEW: Series C and D, plus the first ten verses in Series E.
- Complete the topic and reference quiz on page 70.
- Read "How to Keep Learning and Reviewing" on page 73.

## Questions for Meditation

Galatians 6:9-10 (context: Galatians 6:1-10)

- Who decides when will be the proper time to see the results of our doing good?
- Who should benefit from our good works?

Matthew 5:16 (context: Matthew 5:1-16)

- How does the truth of this passage relate to James 2:14-17?

## Meditation and Review

# Topic and Reference Quiz

Use the blank spaces to fill in the series names, the topics, and the references for the complete *Topical Memory System*.

A. _____

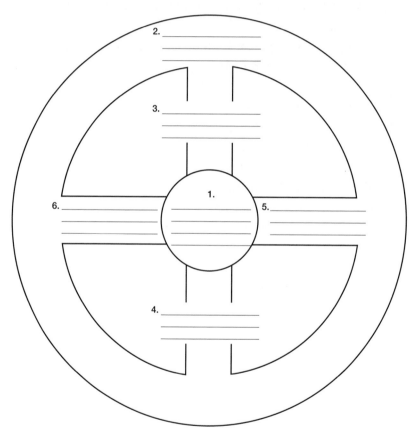

B. _____

3. _____

**MANKIND**                             **GOD**

1. _____

5. _____

2. _____

6. _____

4. _____

**DEATH**                             **LIFE**

C. _____

1. _____

_____         _____

2. _____

_____         _____

3. _____

_____         _____

4. _____

_____         _____

5. _____

_____         _____

6. _____

_____         _____

D. _____

    1. _____

    _____    _____

    2. _____

    _____    _____

    3. _____

    _____    _____

    4. _____

    _____    _____

    5. _____

    _____    _____

    6. _____

    _____    _____

E. _____

    1. _____

    _____    _____

    2. _____

    _____    _____

    3. _____

    _____    _____

    4. _____

    _____    _____

    5. _____

    _____    _____

    6. _____

    _____    _____

# How to Keep Learning and Reviewing

**Keep Reviewing**

God has given us a "forgetter," so you must continue reviewing the verses you have learned in order to retain them. A simple, workable review system will help you.

For the first few weeks after memorizing Series E, you will especially want to concentrate on reviewing those twelve verses. Here's a simple plan you can follow for the first four weeks:

- Week 1 — Daily review: Series A, B, and E.
- Week 2 — Daily review: Series C, D, and E.
- Week 3 — Daily review: Series A, B, and E.
- Week 4 — Daily review: Series C, D, and E.

After the fourth week, you may want to review one of the five series each day on Monday through Friday: Series A on Monday, Series B on Tuesday, and so on through the week.

Don't lose what you have worked so hard to obtain! Be faithful in reviewing your verses.

**Use the "Buddy System"**

Self-discipline is hard, so try to find someone to help you in reviewing your memorized verses regularly. This "buddy" could be your spouse or one of your children, or a friend or coworker.

## What about Learning New Verses?

You may already have a list of verses for future memory — verses that have impressed you from your devotional time, from a sermon, or from a conversation with a friend who shared the verse with you. You will want to continue memorizing and meditating on key Bible portions, so the Holy Spirit will have them at his disposal to use in your life and ministry.

Set a goal now of learning and meditating on one, two, or three new verses each week. You can place these under the same topics you learned in the *Topical Memory System*, or you can give them new topic titles of your own choosing.

Be sure to continually revise your review system to include regular review of the new verses you are learning.

## Expanding Your Review System

As you learn more and more verses it will naturally take more time and effort to review them and to keep them all sharp in your memory. Having a systematic review plan will become increasingly important.

One of the simplest foundations for a good review system is to arrange all your verses according to the books of the Bible, rather than according to topics, with all the verses within a book arranged according to chapter and verse.

To help you begin such a system, the verses in the *Topical Memory System* are arranged on the next page according to this plan.

Leviticus 19:11
Numbers 23:19
Joshua 1:8
Psalm 119:9,11
Proverbs 3:9-10
Isaiah 26:3
Isaiah 41:10
Isaiah 53:6
Lamentations 3:22-23
Matthew 4:19
Matthew 5:16
Matthew 6:33
Matthew 28:19-20
Mark 10:45
Luke 9:23
John 1:12
John 5:24
John 13:34-35
John 14:21
John 15:7
Acts 1:8
Acts 24:16
Romans 1:16
Romans 3:23
Romans 4:20-21
Romans 5:8
Romans 6:23
Romans 8:32
Romans 12:1
Romans 12:2
1 Corinthians 2:12
1 Corinthians 3:16
1 Corinthians 15:58

2 Corinthians 4:5
2 Corinthians 5:17
2 Corinthians 9:6-7
Galatians 2:20
Galatians 6:9-10
Ephesians 2:8-9
Ephesians 5:3
Philippians 2:3-4
Philippians 4:6-7
Philippians 4:13
Philippians 4:19
2 Timothy 3:16
Titus 3:5
Hebrews 2:18
Hebrews 9:27
Hebrews 10:24-25
Hebrews 11:6
Hebrews 12:3
1 Peter 2:11
1 Peter 3:18
1 Peter 5:5-6
1 Peter 5:7
1 John 1:3
1 John 2:15-16
1 John 3:18
1 John 5:13
Revelation 3:20

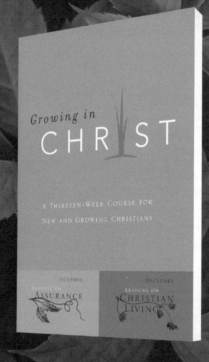

## THE NAVIGATORS® STORY

◑

T HANK YOU for picking up this NavPress book! I hope it has been a blessing to you.

NavPress is a ministry of The Navigators. The Navigators began in the 1930s, when a young California lumberyard worker named Dawson Trotman was impacted by basic discipleship principles and felt called to teach those principles to others. He saw this mission as an echo of 2 Timothy 2:2: "And the things you have heard me say in the presence of many witnesses entrust to reliable people who will also be qualified to teach others" (NIV).

In 1933, Trotman and his friends began discipling members of the US Navy. By the end of World War II, thousands of men on ships and bases around the world were learning the principles of spiritual multiplication by the intentional, person-to-person teaching of God's Word.

After World War II, The Navigators expanded its relational ministry to include college campuses; local churches; the Glen Eyrie Conference Center and Eagle Lake Camps in Colorado Springs, Colorado; and neighborhood and citywide initiatives across the country and around the world.

Today, with more than 2,600 US staff members—and local ministries in more than 100 countries—The Navigators continues the transformational process of making disciples who make more disciples, advancing the Kingdom of God in a world that desperately needs the hope and salvation of Jesus Christ and the encouragement to grow deeper in relationship with Him.

NAVPRESS was created in 1975 to advance the calling of The Navigators by bringing biblically rooted and culturally relevant products to people who want to know and love Christ more deeply. In January 2014, NavPress entered an alliance with Tyndale House Publishers to strengthen and better position our rich content for the future. Through *THE MESSAGE* Bible and other resources, NavPress seeks to bring positive spiritual movement to people's lives.

*If you're interested in learning more or becoming involved with The Navigators, go to www.navigators.org. For more discipleship content from The Navigators and NavPress authors, visit www.thedisciplemaker.org. May God bless you in your walk with Him!*

*Sincerely,*

DON PAPE
VP/PUBLISHER, NAVPRESS

NavPress

www.navpress.com

CP1308